That's why we can

be so sure that every

detail in our lives

of love for God

is worked into

something good.

Romans 8:28 (MSG)

STRENGTHENING

Decision-Making

and

Governance

Supporting New Expeditions

Blake Bradford

the greatest
EXPEDITION

STRENGTHENING
Decision-Making and Governance
Supporting New Expeditions

**Scripture quotations taken from
the Holy Bible**

MSG
Scripture taken from The Message.
Copyright © 1993, 1994, 1995, 1996, 2000, 2001, 2002.
Used by permission of NavPress Publishing Group.

NIV
Scripture quotations taken from The Holy Bible, New International Version®
NIV® Copyright © 1973, 1978, 1984, 2011 by Biblica, Inc.™
Used by permission. All rights reserved worldwide.

This resource was commissioned as
one of many interconnected steps in the
journey of *The Greatest Expedition*.

GreatestExpedition.com

the greatest
EXPEDITION

Table of Contents

Foreword

This resource was commissioned as one of many interconnected steps in the journey of *The Greatest Expedition*. While each step is important individually, we intentionally built the multi-step Essentials Pack and the Expansion Pack to provide a richer and fuller experience with the greatest potential for transformation and introducing more people to a relationship with Jesus Christ. For more information, visit GreatestExpedition.org.

However, we also recognize you may be exploring this resource apart from *The Greatest Expedition*. You might find yourself on a personal journey, a small group journey, or perhaps a church leadership team journey. We are so glad you are on this journey!

As you take each step in your expedition, your Expedition Team will discover whether the ministry tools you will be exploring will be utilized only for the Expedition Team or if this expedition will be a congregational journey. Our hope and prayer is *The Greatest Expedition* is indeed a congregational journey, but if it proves to be a solo journey for just the Expedition Team, God will still do amazing things through your intentional exploration, discernment, and faithful next steps.

Regardless of how you came to discover *The Greatest Expedition*, it will pave the way to a new God-inspired expedition. Be brave and courageous on your journey through *The Greatest Expedition!*

Kay L Kotan, PCC

Director, *The Greatest Expedition*

INTRODUCTION
Let's Get Going!
Uh...Who Brought the Map?

Our church was stuck. Our core leaders, who made up our congregation's expedition team, could (sort of) imagine the destination, but the distance from the *now* to the *there* felt incredibly, overwhelming, far. The very thought of the journey itself incapacitated us. In an early gathering of the Caravan that our Expedition Teams formed together with leaders in other churches, we sat at our team's table, hearing some of the journeys that our neighboring churches were taking.

And we felt stuck.

John, our Expedition Guide, drew a rudimentary map on the dry erase board, "Have you ever taken a road trip to the Grand Canyon with the family? You can't get there in one day. It will take several, especially with a car full of kids. What do you need to decide?"

Beth answered, "Well, we need to decide if we want to go through Texas or Oklahoma on our way – that decision will make a huge difference." Richard had traveled out west and knew that fuel stations were much more spread apart than the denser area that we called home, so one couldn't expect to just 'happen' upon a rare gas station right when you needed it. Misty knew that the kids wouldn't want to spend all day buckled up in the car- the parents would need to plan trip legs that included fun activities along the way.

Finally, Richard picked up a thick binder, worn on the corners and filled to the brim, and exclaimed, "I've got 40 years of church plans, vision statements, and goals in this folder. They all describe our final destination – our 'Grand Canyon' – but we never drew a map that showed us the first gas station on our trip." It was an insight that was worth the whole training experience for our team. Richard's observation unlocked our particular congregation's issue in that season: our Expedition Team needed to create shorter-term, attainable goals.

Now we got to work! While we always had God's big vision – that final destination – in mind, our journey mattered, too. We needed to look at every ministry, governance decision, and choice as if they were travel stops and gas stations on our journey toward that vision God had for the congregation. As a young minister serving my first "solo pastorate" and seeking to encourage our leadership team, I was amazed at the ability of our leaders to be creative, mission-focused, and utilize our larger vision to navigate the day-to-day decisions about ministry.

Governance matters in congregations. Good governance in nonprofit organizations, such as churches, means building accountability throughout the system and creating a decision-making culture for the congregation. The governing leadership board (church council, administrative board, etc.) is accountable to Jesus Christ for the mission. The pastor is accountable to the board as a partner in vision-casting and vision-interpreting, guiding the process of connecting goals to the bigger vision and sharing the story of God's goals for the congregation. The ministry leaders (and staff) are accountable to the pastor for fulfilling the objectives that tie into the goals. These short-term objectives and larger God-sized goals are the travel stops and gas stations on your greatest expedition as you journey. (You'll dive deep into how to make all of this work using strategic planning in the following resource.)

Strengthening the decision-making process is one of the steps your congregation will need to be effective and fruitful. Church governance is complex, and a host of issues from church size, matriarch/patriarch issues, local culture, congregational history, and pastoral history come into play when defining a particular church's culture, much less about changing the church's culture.

Even considering all these contextual issues that create such complexity in different faith communities, what is similar for most congregations is that the governance system that today's leaders have inherited is not suited for the opportunities and challenges that congregations face today. I am writing this resource in the summer of 2020 in the middle of a global pandemic. To respond to the health emergency, churches had to make a series of radical decisions extremely quickly.

The governing model for most mainline denominations was explicitly designed to slow down the decision-making processes. The legacy model of governance is for multiple governing committees to meet (always in person), work through questions, send them to a church council, perhaps have questions sent back to numerous other committees. Then the committee members are usually also the ones mobilizing the ministry to be done. Some congregations even have inherited a bicameral governing system in which leadership is divided between an Administrative Board (responsible for finances, facilities, staffing, and resources) and a separate Council on Ministries (responsible for programs and ministries). To get anything approved, an idea must survive both governing bodies.

These inherited systems were born out of the post-war era when the church's goals were often assumed, growth was assumed, volunteerism was assumed, and the church's role in the greater culture was assumed. Perfectly created for that era and culture, these layers of committee structures were designed to slowly examine any potential change and not "rock the boat."

Today's context for congregations couldn't be more different. While the legacy structures we inherited are exquisitely designed to make sure nothing new ever happens, the leadership structures that we need today must be nimble, adaptive decision-making groups that are designed to hold us accountable to Jesus' mission and unleash more disciples to *be engaged* in ministry, not just attend meetings *about* ministry.

CHAPTER ONE
Governance and Mobilization

This resource will refer to the term "governance" throughout its pages. Let me begin by defining what governance in a church is, using three primary categories:

- **Stewardship:** The board tends to the fiduciary responsibilities and alignment of God's people and resources. This could include ensuring the facility is adequately insured and safe, that personnel policies are appropriately followed, and that the church's finances are regularly audited to ensure that the treasurer is properly handling the congregation's money.

  The board's fiduciary leadership is not just "bureaucracy looking for meaning" or a distraction from "real ministry." Members of the leadership board, as fiduciaries, have certain legal, ethical , and denominational responsibilities. If our churches and communities cannot trust that we will be good stewards in the worldly concerns of financial obligations, matters of safety and liability, and sound governance, then why would we think anyone would listen to us when we attempt to share our witness of the Good News of Jesus?

- **Discernment and Strategic Work:** This is the creative, adaptive, and innovative work of discerning God's dreams for the congregation, working to set the congregation's next steps and seeing that resources are aligned with those priorities.

- **Accountable Leadership:** Governance is also concerned with setting a culture of well-aligned, impact-focused ministry.

  Kingdom impact must be the leadership board's first objective, and it is from this missional purpose that the board then partners with the pastor and leaders to build systems for planning, implementing and evaluating impactful ministries.

As your Expedition Team considers its governance systems, it is best to figure out some metaphorical heuristics to describe the work of church leadership. These mental shortcuts will help your team not only conceptualize the work that each part of your leadership needs to accomplish but using a shared language also keeps your committees and teams staying in their lane as time goes on.

Dan Enwhitle, the Senior Executive Director at The United Methodist Church of the Resurrection, teaches leadership principles. One of the metaphors he has used for years imprinted itself upon my vocabulary. If you think of a bicycle, it has two parts you interact with: the pedals and the handlebars. The pedals are for pedaling – for action – for getting somewhere. The handlebars are for steering. If one thinks of different ways that church leadership is lived out, there are particular roles for both pedaling and steering. Some committees and teams are all about pedaling, and some committees' roles are focused on steering. In this metaphor, the pedals are ministry mobilization – discipleship and community transformation. The handlebars are about governance – steering the church toward its mission, setting the direction, casting the vision, making God-sized goals, exploring potential new expeditions, and holding us accountable to the MAP (ministry action plans).

Without steering, you pedal into a ditch. Without pedaling, you will go nowhere fast, no matter which way you are pointed. The single board is about the work of steering – governance. There should be plenty of ministry teams and small groups pedaling hard to do the ministry. Still, when the Leadership Board meets, they are focused on accountability to the mission of Christ, making policies and decisions, and setting the church's direction. Separating the work of steering and pedaling is the first act in taking control of your decision-making and governance system.

There are plenty of jokes about church committees having meetings about light bulbs and running toilets. By separating the functions of governance and mobilization, your board's job is not about the light bulbs but instead about ensuring that the maintenance team leader is held accountable for fulfilling her responsibility for lighting and plumbing. The distinction matters and a board's effectiveness can be judged on how well it sticks to its steering role and avoids the temptation of becoming a fast-pedaling ministry team.

Once church leaders understand that these roles are equally necessary and important but very different, I suggest that leaders utilize the metaphor to stay on track. I have been in meetings where the leaders all know about this heuristic. It is great to see one board member pull the meeting back on track by saying, *"Hey, I think we are getting into pedaling work – let's get our hands back on the handlebars,"* or a ministry team leader says, *"that question is more about policy and sounds like a steering question, not a mobilization question. I will send a note to the board and see if we can get clarity on that."*

A common leadership language will keep the board from attempting to micromanage the work of ministry teams and staff. It will also remind staff and ministry teams that the board's responsibility is to steer the trajectory, allocate resources, and evaluate missional effectiveness. The bike metaphor encourages empathy and clarity as board members and staff/ministry team leaders seek to accomplish Christ's vision together.

Let's use this metaphor to unpack a pivotal moment in early church history. In Acts chapter 6, the fledgling church was struggling, and things had gotten messy. As the church grew, its ability to scale up its ministries had run out of steam. A workforce and resource allocation problem had cropped up. The Greek-speaking widows were being left out in the daily distribution of food. The Hellenist faction of the church was getting mad at the Hebrew faction. The Apostles had been trying to maintain both the steering and the pedaling roles, and they simply couldn't pedal fast enough and still fulfill their responsibilities to share the Word of God. Relationships among the disciples had begun to deteriorate, folks were feeling left out, and the Apostles were distracted from their important task of strategic leadership. I'm sure somebody wrote the district superintendent a scathing email and included a petition.

So, they called a church-wide meeting and suggested a new path. No longer would both the governance and ministry mobilization roles be hoarded in the single group of Apostles. The body would choose seven trustworthy and faithful leaders to care for the poor and mobilize the church's ministry. The Apostles would be held accountable to do the "steering" work of the fledgling church. The Apostles laid hands and commissioned these deacons for their "pedaling" work, and now, the church was organized to evangelize, grow, and impact lives, communities, and the larger world. The end of the biblical passage shows us what happens when we stop hoarding ministry in a few leaders and instead organize our churches to enable ministry to flourish:

> *The Word of God prospered. The number of disciples in Jerusalem increased dramatically. Not least, a great many priests submitted themselves to the faith.*
>
> **Acts 6:7 (MSG)**

Strengthening the decision-making and governance systems of a congregation is not about efficiency for its own sake. It's also not about "rearranging the deck chairs on the Titanic" just to look busy when you don't know what else to do. I propose that healthy, efficient, agile, accountable, and adaptive leadership structures ultimately enable the

Word of God to prosper, encourage and enable ministry to reach people with impact and reach new people for Jesus. This work in this generation requires us to change the way we have historically organized and steered our congregations. Bike metaphor in hand, the next chapter will help you imagine an innovative way to structure the steering portion of your leadership.

CHAPTER TWO
Better...Stronger...Faster...

As I shared in the introduction, our legacy church committee leadership structures simply were not designed for our era. They were formulated in a post-war era of unprecedented church growth. They thrived when American culture and church attendance (especially mainline Protestant church attendance) appeared to go hand-in-hand.

Civic clubs and masonic lodges thrived in the same era, using many of the same committee-based governance frameworks. Responsibility and authority were spread out in numerous committees amongst leaders (mostly male) who shared a similar worldview. Businesses and churches made ten and twenty year plans that were very institution-focused.

True or not, the leaders of the era thought the primary challenge of churches was managing growth during the post-war boom. This does not describe today's culture, in which diverse groups of church leaders seek to lead congregations as missional movements into a complex cultural marketplace of ideas, technologies, and commitments. The legacy leadership structures we have inherited are simply not designed for a missional movement. We need creative, evangelistic, Apostolic leaders who are empowered and enabled to make nimble, innovative decisions in a fast-moving world.

In a leadership training seminar I attended in the early 2000s, I was shocked to hear how large corporations had recently moved from 10-year to 3-year strategic plans. Now those same international corporations have long-term plans that only look ahead 18 months! I was initially trained to take congregations through multi-year strategic planning processes. Nowadays, we are lapped by our changing world while our strategic planning team is still tying up the laces on their running shoes.

Underneath these concerns about efficient decision-making is a more profound concern. As a church judicatory official and former congregational coach, I have seen individuals and committees build power centers that create internal opposition to one another. The finance committee tries to underfund the Trustees; the personnel committee sets salaries and adds staff positions without bothering to ask the treasurer what the church can afford; the weekday childcare program tries to tell the Sunday school group which rooms may be used for discipleship classes. Multiple committees ripping the handlebars out of each other's hands doesn't bode well for missional alignment or efficiency.

So, what can be done? How can congregations restructure to lead and govern the church, make decisions, and be accountable stewards of all the congregation's resources, people, and ministry?

As a Gen-X kid, I loved to watch reruns of the *Six Million Dollar Man*. Colonel Steve Austin may have been injured in a crash of his experimental plane, but with some bionic upgrades, he became a secret agent who saved the world every week in under an hour, with commercials. I remember the tagline: "We can rebuild him. We have the technology. We can make him better than he was. Better... stronger...faster."

It's past time to rebuild our decision-making and governance. And this time, we need to get bionic! In our case, going "bionic" does not mean adding layers of complex systems. Instead, effective and missional leadership comes not from creating more complexity but through simplification. One of the most straightforward ways to "get bionic" – to create a clear process for better, stronger governance and faster decision-making – is to transition to what is commonly referred to as the *one-board model*, but what I call the *simplified, accountable leadership structure.*

One way to do this, especially for the small church, is to go simple: A single board of six to eleven members that serve simultaneously as Personnel Committee (Staff Parish Relations Committee for United Methodists), Finance Committee, Trustees (responsible for property, insurance, and liability), and the Executive Committee (Administrative Board or Church Council) will enable your church to:

- Unleash lay leaders from the committee room to make disciples of Jesus

- Focus on the mission field instead of "turf wars"

- Align people and resources to fulfill your ministry plan

- Reduce bureaucracy and meetings

- Shift from "representatives" to missional leadership (Members of the Leadership Board should not come to the table to "represent the choir" or the food pantry team or any particular constituency. Instead, every member is accountable first to Jesus' mission for the church. Other than the pastor, you should also not include staff as members of the board but invite them as guests on an as-needed basis.)

Of course, fewer people making decisions is NOT the goal of moving to a simplified, accountable leadership structure. The goal of any change in structure must ultimately be about successfully implementing the Christ-centered mission of the congregation to more effectively make disciples. You need a governing and strategic structure that will help make this holy mission a reality.

As a regional denominational leader in a mainline church with a large percentage of tiny congregations, I have seen plenty of applications from churches seeking to move toward simple governance because the number of active members does not allow for filling all the disciplinary committees as separate entities. While a simplified structure may help to solve that dilemma, it should never be the ultimate purpose. I have also rejected applications from congregations seeking to move toward a single leadership board to sideline critics of the pastor.

Simplifying your structure is not about consolidating power. It is about making the congregation's decision-making nimbler and unleashing lay leadership for more ministry! Kay Kotan and I offer a warning that we shared in our book, *Impact! Reclaiming the Call of Lay Ministry:*

> *Changing the number of people around the leadership table without also changing the leadership culture will only result in an isolated and ineffective board"* (pp 114-115).[1]

Kay Kotan and Blake Bradford

Healthy motivations matter when you are seeking to simplify. While very small churches may choose to simplify into a single board because they cannot field a whole roster of committees, mid-size and larger congregations will approach the question with a mix of

---

[1] Kay Kotan and Blake Bradford. *Impact! Reclaiming the Call of Lay Ministry.* Market Square Books: Knoxville. 2018.

motivations. Most churches considering a simplification in leadership and decision-making structures base these changes on one or more of five driving motivators:

- Efficiency

- Alignment

- Missional focus

- Accountability

- Adaptability

Efficiency

In its traditional structure, many church decisions must run through multiple committees, usually requiring numerous months to approve a single decision. Many times, churches have all their members tied up in administrative tasks leaving no one left to do the mobilization part of ministry! The more disciples you have with hands gripping the handlebars and steering the church, the fewer are left to pedal – to transform the community and world for Jesus. So, I am a proponent of rightsizing your leadership and structure to fit your reality.

In my last appointment as a congregational coach, I did some conflict work for a congregation. They had all the committees that had existed in their golden era in the mid-1980s when the church was 400% larger. Now, the same generation of leaders was in charge, but the kids had moved off, the church had aged, and the congregation had shrunk. But they still had all the committees attempting to function, and there were meetings almost every day of the week – and way too many ineffective ministries, and they were exhausted and ineffective.

As I looked at the system, I saw a mirror image of a church I had served very early in my ministry. The district superintendent said it worshiped 90. When I arrived, they laughed and said, "No, that's Easter. We've got 60 in worship on a good day." But we got focused on doing a few ministries well, and they grew. When we got to 125 in average worship and a few hundred on the roll in only a couple of years, we noticed the opposite problem – we were still organized as a small family church for 60. Ministry experiments could be easily bottlenecked because our steering and pedaling were all done by the same group of folks. It was like parents buying their teenage son new school uniform pants in August, only to discover by "long-pants season" in October, that a growth spurt made his new long trousers look like knee pants.

Efficient rightsizing means having a leadership structure that can make decisions with agility and respects your parishioners' gifts and time.

How would you rate the efficiency of the decision-making in your local church? What aspects are working well, and where is the efficiency lacking?

Alignment

Most churches find themselves working in silos. One team or committee has no idea what the other is doing. Sometimes scheduling or resource conflicts arise. There is internal competition for people power, funding, and staff time. Groups do not seem to all be pulling in the same direction for a common purpose or focus. Some churches often operate as multiple mini-churches or groups within one church.

Alignment with the mission and vision is about being faithful to our disciple-making and world-transforming purpose – it is not about reaching a consensus. Alignment to our mission and vision needs to be non-negotiable. One problem with our inherited multiple-committee structure is that it creates too many independent and myopic power silos, with none having the ability to look at the larger picture creatively. A simple leadership board can utilize all the resources (staffing, finances, facilities) simultaneously to address opportunities and challenges while keeping the large picture in focus.

How would you rate the missional alignment of resources in your local church? What aspects are working well, and where is the alignment lacking?

Missional Focus

The attractional, "build it, and they will come" model of doing church was on its last legs when the 2020 pandemic hit. It was only still viable amongst a few very large churches in a few regions of the country. It depended upon a consumerist mindset, endless catalog of programs, large budgets, and a culture of church membership expectations. Instead of spiritual leaders and equippers of disciples to spread the Gospel, pastors were expected to be chaplains to the members. A survey of church members to discover the role of the church would probably get many answers like: "to help me grow in my faith," "to provide pastoral care," and "to fill me up when I feel empty." These consumerist answers make the church sound more like a spiritual club rather than the Body of Christ on a mission.

At a 2015 School of Congregational Development, the late United Methodist Bishop Michael Conyer lamented, "We went from being fishers of people to tenders of aquariums!" Structure won't solve the problem of missional focus. Still, it certainly can create a clear pathway for the church's leadership to truly hold themselves and the larger church accountable as it steers the congregation onward on its disciple-making mission of Jesus. A single leadership board with appropriate authority, accountability, and voice can keep the entire church focused on Christ's mission.

How would you rate the missional focus of your local church? Where is the mission in focus and out of focus?

Accountability

When I was a congregational coach, I often asked the pastor and lay leaders about the relationship between authority and responsibility in the congregation. Sadly, I have observed too many situations in which the two were tenuously connected, if at all. I also remember asking a leader who was responsible for a particular ministry, and he said, "Well, we all sort of team up for that. It's less about titles and job descriptions; we just get it done. So I guess everyone is responsible."

While I understand and sympathize with the sentiment, it is hard to hold "everyone accountable" for a project. If everyone is responsible, no one is responsible. Accountability is not about finding someone to blame, but it is about connecting responsibility and authority. While these examples are about staffing, clear accountability is even more important for governing committees.

We have all been members of committees in which it was unclear if the Trustees or Finance Committee needed to approve something first and the Executive Committee kept referring an issue to a different committee, or perhaps when two committees vehemently disagreed and one team's inaction meant the other team's failure. These are all signs that your structure is not supporting accountability.

How would you rate the efficiency of the decision-making in your local church? What aspects are working well, and where is the efficiency lacking?

Adaptability

I still remember one of my most dispiriting staff meetings. After several weeks of sharing about the church's new vision and talking about the virtues of creativity, new opportunities for collaboration, and adjusting to the curve balls thrown at us, all the directors were supposed to come with their proposed ministry calendars for the year.

One of the staff brought a list of events, first printed several years ago, with a series of new dates handwritten in the margin. Upon closer expectation, it was a series of dates scratched out and written, and scratched out and written, and scratched out and written. Year after year, the director had simply done ministry planning by photocopier, making allowances only to the changes of the current calendar.

Meeting today's realities requires a lot more creativity than a photocopier. To be fruitful and effective, your Expedition Team will need to be able to adapt, create, and adjust. There have been many books written about adaptive leadership, both secular and church-related. Tod Bolsinger has gifted the church with an excellent metaphor of "canoeing the mountains" by comparing the adaptive leadership to the explorations of Lewis and Clark as they created the map of the west for the young U.S. government. They had expected to find a river that would flow to the Pacific Ocean. Still, instead they had to figure a way to turn their canoeing skills into mountaineering skills when they ran into the Rockies (see Bolsinger's *Canoeing the Mountains: Christian Leadership in Uncharted Territory*).

In spring 2020, almost every church in America suddenly, with a few days' notice, had to adapt: from ministries designed to huddle together people in intimate settings to becoming online worshiping and discipling communities. I had to learn a new sentence: "Our primary worship service is online, but we are also offering several intimate, socially distant, and safe in-person worship experiences throughout the week. Please bring your own mask." I did not learn that particular string of words in seminary. Very few of our preachers were trained to be televangelists, but adaptation was vital, not only for institutional survival but for missional fruitfulness. We all learned a powerful lesson – the inherited, multiple-month process of decision-making would no longer work. To be fruitful during a pandemic, adaptive leadership in churches meant that congregations would either succumb to unsustainable pastoral authoritarianism or create simpler systems of lay leadership decision-making. Rapid cultural change is not going away. For lay leadership to thrive, nurture creativity, maintain accountability, and be adaptive, simpler structures must be enthusiastically invited into our congregations.

How would you rate the adaptability in your local church? What aspects are working well, and where is the adaptability lacking?

CHAPTER THREE
Challenges To A Change

Challenges, conflict and anxiety are a given in any community. It is no one's particular fault – conflict just *is*. I often tell groups that conflict is Biblical – Jesus tells us how to address conflict in Matthew 18, The Book of Acts has several occasions of the early church trying to figure balance the competing demands of the mission and the diverse new church community, and huge chunks of the New Testament letters are devoted to managing different groups of believers annoyed with each other. In a healthy congregation, conflict is actually expected as part of the creative process of missional creativity, and must be reframed from "competing sides trying to win at all costs because the church's future is at stake" into "challenges to be overcome by the team serving in ministry together."

However, in a season in which the

congregation is climbing out of a brutal global pandemic, a time when the Christian Church's perceived role in the community facing huge demographic changes, with denominational fracturing, and with polarization becoming the norm in every aspect of culture, anxiety is as palpable as it is to be expected. High anxiety breeds a whole new level of organizational challenges, including mistrust, a theology of scarcity, and fear of failure. In this context, missional creativity can be lost in the attempt to maintain stability in the face of anxiety. With intentionality and communication, however, creative challenges can be transformed into creative opportunities. I recommend a leadership board address challenges through some particular lenses:

- Relying on **Christ as our Center**

- Modeling an impact-focused **Community**

- Defining **Clarity in Committee Roles and Structure**

- Encouraging **Creative Collaboration** among all parties

My co-author Kay Kotan and I both teach workshops focused on our book, *Mission Possible: A Simple Structure for Missional*

Effectiveness, helping congregational teams in transitioning from their inherited complex committee structures into a simplified, accountable leadership structure, often called the "one-board model" of governance.

In those workshops, we usually start by doing a reality check. We ask, "How many people in your congregation are members of a governing committee?" We get answers from 25-50 to even 100 folks as members of governing boards! I have seen a congregation with 50 worshiping members have over 50 leadership and committee positions. It is a part-time church with a bi-vocational, quarter-time pastor, and all she has time for is sermon writing and attending redundant meetings.

But meetings are not ministry!

Meetings are great – we can use them to create ministry action plans, hold ourselves and others accountable, cast the vision, equip, make decisions and policies, and stay connected spiritually as a team. But let's not forget that every hour a disciple is at the meeting table, an hour is lost from ministry in the mission field, building new Christ-centered relationships, or growing disciples.

Meetings are great, and we need to keep

some perspective. Meetings accomplish many things, but meetings are not ministry. This concept is difficult for a member whose identity – sometimes their sense of self – might be wrapped up in holding the same church office for decades, or who doesn't feel particularly gifted in leading ministries and prefers the administration of the church (I actually would call that a spiritual issue).

To stay in missional alignment, committees need to be Christ-centered, not focused on turf or perceived power. When churches hand out offices and roles to placate certain families or constituencies, it distracts from the difficult work of servant leadership. Bob is not on the Leadership Board to represent the choir. And Bob, along with every member of the board, is responsible first to the mission of Jesus Christ. The board should represent the entire church as it seeks faithfulness and fruitfulness in this mission.

While one could look at a simplified board and think that it shrinks the pool of involvement and leadership, actually, the reverse is true. I believe that people (especially new disciples) today are not looking to fill a slot on a nominations report. Disciples seek to have meaning in their lives and make an impact in the world for Jesus Christ.

Keeping a chair warm on an administrative committee which has no real responsibility or authority does not bring meaning into their life, and neither does cumbersome decision-making processes. If it takes too long for a ministry idea to become a ministry reality, today's leaders will drop out. Twenty-first-century disciples want to see how their participation in ministry is growing new disciples or changing lives. This was always the case.

Rodney Steele, one of the senior pastor mentors I served alongside, told me a story from early in his ministry. During his time as a pastor of a small rural church in Arkansas, he was sharing about how Heifer International sent chickens across the globe to help families create sustainable livelihoods. One of his members at this fundraising event said, "OK, preacher, show me the chickens." Rodney was at a loss for words and tried to answer her, but she was clear with her expectations. Saying, "Preacher, you want me to help send chickens around the world. I want to see the chickens. I want to hear them cluck." Good lesson! We all want to hear the chickens cluck. We all want to know that our discipleship has meaning and is making an impact for Jesus.

By making leadership service real and meaningful, the pool of possible leaders actually increases. By shifting more leadership from committees that "steer the bike" to teams that pedal and mobilize ministry, your church is enlarging the number of leaders hungry to serve and the entire discipleship apparatus of the church. Steering does not create ministry and missional momentum. Only pedaling creates momentum.

Simpler governance and decision-making structures are also challenging in churches with gigantic governing boards that expect a quarterly Board of Stewards Meeting with seating for sixty members, plus spouses, a dinner, and an evening's worth of presentations punctuated by occasional voting make the whole thing feel vaguely democratic. But these huge boards are hurting your church.

- First, this structure tells members that "important" leadership in the church is more about attending board meetings than engaging in ministry. Simplifying your church's governing and decision-making process – the steering function – allows more disciples to be unleashed to mobilize ministries. As I shared above, today's disciples are seeking meaning. Membership on a board that only involves a chicken dinner and pro forma voting will not create the meaning or impact today's disciples crave.

- Second, huge boards are unable to make critical decisions necessary to govern. The COVID pandemic showed us how ministry conditions today require a quick response and hands-on leadership. Brainstorming, innovation, creativity, and agility are not hallmarks of groups of humans larger than a dozen.

- The third problem is accountability. Churches with gigantic boards often believe that their boards signal democracy, ignoring that the large boards actually signal that a small group of unelected insiders or sometimes only the staff are setting the agenda and making all the decisions. "Well, the Board of Stewards approved it" is an answer without meaning – it tells me nothing about the work that went into a decision or policy. Huge boards usually devolve into rubber stamps that diffuse accountability and are utterly lacking the capacity to be agile, informed decision-making bodies. Simple structures with clear lines of responsibility and authority bring the agenda-setting and decision-making work from the back room into the sunshine.

As a denominational leader, I am often

called after a problem crops up. So, even as a proponent of this simplified, accountable leadership structure, I ask that leaders take the transition process patiently and intentionally. First of all, there are sometimes quite a few emotions built into leadership positions in a local church. Even without a structure change, strengthening decision-making and governance can be difficult in a congregation with well-worn ministry and leadership grooves (aka stuck in a rut). While the presenting issue may be structural, the real problem may be one of identity and emotion. So, be prepared to respond with empathy and clarity when congregation members express a lack of trust, fear of change, misunderstanding of the model, misunderstanding of the purpose, lack of transparency, lack of leadership adaptability, unwillingness for leaders to give up their seat, fear of the unknown, and the perception of the power of the church being in too few hands.

As an Expedition Team, you have spent hours poring through the resources, building ministry action plans, and downloading charts and checklists. You have worked with your Navigator and the Expedition Guide. You have invested in learning and growing as leaders. You have discerned your missional purpose, and you understand the governance architecture of the structure you are building. Your average church member has not done this homework. So, take the time to work through the fears and misunderstandings. You may have heard the quote often attributed to Abraham Lincoln: "Give me six hours to chop down a tree, and I will spend the first four sharpening the ax." Allow some time to sharpen the ax with the larger congregation and help the entire church, not just the board, understand the motivations and vocabulary of the change.

Investment in this time early in the process will help out later, and not just the emotional reactions to change. At one church early in my ministry, I thought I had embedded a fresh purpose and set of systems, but it was only after I left that I discovered that it was only embedded in the small team, not the larger body – a regret I still carry to this day. While your membership may trust you enough to vote their approval of a new structure, a problem shows up a year or two later, after the first set of leaders rotate off the board or when your pastor is appointed to a new congregation. Then the church is left with a governance system on paper that nobody knows how to run. I have spoken with congregational leaders who have inherited a "sports car of a structure," but nobody in leadership knows how to drive stick.

One additional challenge to change in a church governance system that cannot be overlooked is the relationship of church size to governance. A congregation's size deeply impacts its leadership culture, and the governance style that may work in a megachurch or even a "pastoral-sized" congregation of 75-125 active members will be experienced very differently in a small church. In smaller churches, everyone is always wearing governance and ministry hats simultaneously, adaptations will need to be made so that the governance and fiduciary work of leadership is framed separately from the ministry work, especially in matters with legal or denominational polity implications.

The role of the pastor will also look different in differently-sized congregations. In larger congregations, the lead pastor takes on a stronger vision-casting role with leadership functions (planning, staffing, board development, and stewardship) taking up a greater percentage of the pastor's time. In mid-sized churches, the pastor and the board will always be needing to negotiate and clarify their respective roles and responsibilities, with "governance" and "management" feeling like points on a spectrum rather than a clear-cut binary. For instance, while the pastor may have the "right" to terminate an employee in the by-laws, the reality is that prior notice to the board and the presence of a member of the board or the personnel committee may be expected for any disciplinary action with an employee. The role of the pastor in a small church is particularly different from that expressed in many church leadership books, in that small church pastors who attempt to be the vision-casters, CEO, or ministry managers will soon discover that they have overplayed their hand. In a fall 2021 article I wrote for Ministry Matters, I offered a different metaphor to explain the leadership role of the pastor in the small church's decision-making process:

> *The smaller the church, the more the pastor's leadership exists outside the committee meeting room or even behind the pulpit. Instead the leader rests on the metaphorical porch swing. In my home state, Arkansas, especially in the evening, we enjoy banter from the front porch swing. You sit side-by-side on a porch swing. You can't sit in the adversarial position across from someone, hoping to win*

them over or tire them out. Side-by-side it is,
looking in the same direction, leaning over and
talking with each other, loving each other as
fellow servants of God.[2]

Blake Bradford

In small congregations with an established (but sometimes unelected) matriarch or patriarch, the pastor is more coach than CEO, and pastoral leadership occurs more from the relational "porch swing" than from the board room. By showing respect and curiosity, the pastor can coach key lay leaders as the church's laity make decisions and set priorities.

I encourage congregational leaders and pastors to be in continual conversation together to clarify expectations and boundaries for pastoral authority. Use these clarifying conversations as you create your guiding principles and revisit these principles and expectations on a regular basis so that you can stay on mission, and strike the right balance between accountability and creativity. I'll share more about guiding principles in Chapter Five.

---

[2] Blake Bradford, "Leading the Small Church From the Porch Swing," MinistryMatters.com, October 17,2021.

CHAPTER FOUR
Building a Better Team

In addition to all the ax-sharpening and relational work your Expedition Team may likely need to do to help the larger congregation rethink its governing structures, there are also processes that the church will need to take to transition smoothly. If your Expedition Team discerns that your local church's current decision-making and governance will not be able to support or sustain a new expedition, consider these steps. Following is a 10-step checklist for making a change from inherited legacy structures into a simplified accountable leadership structure. The process should begin with leaders understanding the model, defining their motivators, researching the process, and getting guidance from coaches and denominational leaders on the best way to simplify for their congregation. The process should be transparent, grace-filled, and mission-focused.

10 Steps to Transition to Simplified, Accountable Leadership Structure

(Adapted from Resource-1 of Mission Possible 3+)

1. Determine why a structure change is needed, recommended, or desired. Equip your leaders in basic principles of discernment and accountable leadership. Create a draft timeline and plan for discernment, communication of the proposed change, congregational votes, and launch.

2. Consult your denominational leaders or district superintendent for a preliminary conversation about a potential structure change.
Coaching for your leadership may be available from your regional denominational office or through a certified SAS coach. Create a simplified accountable structure Discernment Team to work with the coach to lead the congregation in learning, organizing, and communicating the discernment process.

3. Ensure the congregation is prepared for an accountable leadership model of governance. Prepare for and lead congregational conversations about potential changes utilizing two-way communication. Lead with the **why** and then follow with the **what** and **how**.

4. Uncover and discuss feedback from the congregation and use the feedback to build your contextually appropriate model for a new leadership structure.

5. Create a temporary task force, approved by the existing administrative board or church

council, to create a draft set of founding guiding principles and to begin preparing updates for all existing congregational policies (personnel, facility, finance, endowment, by-laws, etc.) so that the policies and by-laws will be in compliance with proposed structure.

6. Letter and a coach report is sent to your denominational leader, presiding elder, or district superintendent to officially request a structure change and the convening of a church-wide meeting to approve the new structure.

7. The congregation's separate nominating committee assembles to nominate new leaders illustrating new leadership criteria and structure.

8. An official church-wide meeting, is called with proper notice to approve:

   • New structure

   • Nominations

   • A founding set of guiding principles that the new board is authorized to adapt to meet the ministry and missional needs of the church.

9. Congregational vote of the church-wide body. Once approved, all existing administrative teams cease to exist as separate bodies (this does not include ministry teams) on a certain date set by the church-wide gathering. The church nomination's committee, having been equipped on the new model by a coach, is assigned to produce a new slate of leaders based on the new structure consideration by the church at their annual meeting. Once elected, the

responsibilities and authority of the constituent committees will rest in the new governing board.

10. First meeting of the new board. Elect a trustee/ board of directors chair, orient the board on the guiding principles, and approve a board covenant.

In structuring your new simple model for governance, there are some things to keep in mind. First, a common mistake in describing simplified structure is that "we got rid of all of our committees." Actually, all your committees still exist, but they exist in a single body. Together, all their combined responsibilities constitute the authority of the new leadership board. In other words, the Leadership Board *is* the Finance Committee and *is* the Personnel Committee and *is* the Facility Committee, and *is* the Church Council. Nothing in your denomination's polity book is ignored or removed. Instead, each of the constituent committees' cumulative functions, roles, and responsibilities are all placed upon your new board. It is like every member of the board has several hats sitting in front of them.

As the board moves through its agenda, it will switch hats, from executive committee to property to finances to staffing. Certain agenda topics, such as staff issues or legal negotiations, may require a confidential executive session, but the rest of the meeting is public to members of the congregation.

Below, you will find a chart that outlines a simplified structure with accountable leadership. This chart (using language from Methodist polity) illustrates clear authority, responsibility, and accountability lines.

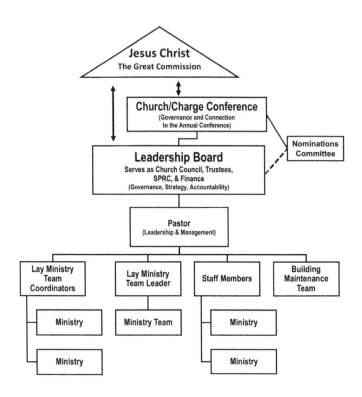

In this structure, the congregation's nominations committee is tasked with the job of recommending persons for only two committees: the governing Leadership Board and Nominations. Some of this may depend on your denomination's polity. For instance, *The United Methodist Book of Discipline* does not allow the duties of the Nominations Committee (of which the pastor serves as chair) to be rolled into the new simplified council/board, so it will continue to exist and serve as a separate body. So, for the most part, these will be the only two standing committees. The only exception for this would be if there is a legally separate church entity such as a Foundation or a weekday childcare board for a state-licensed program.

So, you may be wondering what happens to all the ministry teams if they are not nominated and elected for specific terms like the members of a Leadership Board. They certainly don't disappear. Instead, ministry teams should flourish. While committee and board members are elected, ministry team leaders and members are selected based on their gifts and passion for a particular area of ministry, with no predetermined length of service. Team members are identified, recruited, and equipped by staff (paid or unpaid), team leaders, and/or the pastor. Teams may last only as long as a particular project or may serve on an ongoing basis, with members joining and moving off the team throughout its life. They could be led by a volunteer or a staff member and should ultimately be accountable to the pastor's oversight.

It is suggested that a move to the simplified structure include changing the name of the Leadership Board as well as the names of assorted ministry committees, such as "Worship Committee," to a name that more appropriately describes a ministry team's defined work such as Worship Planning Team, Worship Design Advisory Team, Praise Team, or Worship and Hospitality Team. This helps define the expectations for team members and clarifies the differences between the governance of boards and committees (steering) versus the ministry of teams (mobilization).

Remember, ministry teams are recruited and equipped by the pastor and staff based on the congregation's disciples' gifts, graces, callings, and passions. The ministry teams are all "pedaling together" to accomplish the objectives driven by the church goals. Teams, such as for a specific ministry event or a mission trip, are created and discontinued as needed to accomplish the ministry. Of course, you will still need standing teams for such ministry tasks as hospitality, children/youth ministry, missions, building and grounds, and worship design.

I am often asked if certain skill sets need to be represented on the board, such as an HR professional to provide staffing advice or a contractor or realtor to provide expertise on the facility. While I hope that every disciple on the Leadership Board will bring expertise and life experience to the job of governance, my answer to the question is "no." The members of the Leadership Board should be deeply committed Christians nominated and elected based on their capacity to guide the church and make missional decisions for the church to thrive in its ministry.

There is no board you could construct that would have all the technical expertise necessary to thrive. Therefore, I lean on *ad hoc* task forces, which I call "work teams" to focus on well-defined projects with a clear start and stop date. Each year, a Budget Work Team can be created with a mix of Leadership Board members, finance staff, the pastor, and a few math-and ministry-inclined church members to create a draft budget. Suppose there is a new personnel policy needed. In that case, the Leadership Board can assign a board member or two to lead a process, get church disciples with human resources and legal experience, including some senior church staff, and create a draft policy to present to the Leadership Board. If a global pandemic arrives, a task force with health professionals and public educators could be created to assist the Leadership Board by offering healthy and safe facility recommendations and drafting new policies.

In addition to bringing technical expertise, a short-term work team is a great way to include disciples who might not want to serve a three-year term in governance. Work teams are also perfect training grounds for developing the congregation's future leaders. Through work on a specific project with a set end date, a new love of servant leadership might be kindled, or gifts and talents uncovered.

CHAPTER FIVE
Goals, Giftedness, and Guiding Principles

Earlier resources and Ministry Action Plans in this Great Expedition Series have covered creating a mission, vision, and God-sized goals for the congregation. When leadership moves from legacy structures to a simplified, accountable leadership structure, the church begins to align all its resources to the congregation's mission and unique vision. Those resources include such things as time, energy, people, facility, budget, and calendar. Decisions are made based upon the congregation's mission and vision, as an incarnation of God's spiritual gifts bestowed upon the congregation.

When I was in Boy Scouts growing up (shout out to Troop 198 chartered at Mabelvale United Methodist Church in Arkansas), one of the tasks that I feared the most was not the whitewater paddling or the mountaineering. It was "orienteering." Orienteering is navigating using a map and a compass. It involves math. As a pastor, congregation staff member, and now a district superintendent, everyone I partner with in ministry knows I have a personal rule: I don't do math in public. But, when a patrol of seventh graders are stuck in the middle of the woods with a compass and a map filled with indecipherable hieroglyphs, I suppose one does the best one can.

Orienteering is much like the work of the Leadership Board. Figure out your true north and your ultimate direction (your congregation's mission), plan your steps and control points along the way (goals), and plan how to navigate and adjust for obstacles. You will be hopelessly lost if you don't know your ultimate direction and constantly keep it in mind even as you calculate alterations along your route. In business (including churches), getting lost is sometimes referred to as "mission drift."

While I am a huge fan of signature mission ministries that congregations use to share their story and their passion with the larger community, I always encourage leaders to be on the lookout for mission drift, even in these signature ministries. A few decisions in sequence can get a congregation hopelessly lost. Take the proverbial church "pumpkin patch" as an example. The ministry started as a way for the congregation to go outside their doors, meet the community, and form relationships. The ultimate goal – their true north for this event – was to create opportunities to invite guests into a relationship with Jesus through the church. While the congregation exchanged money for the pumpkins (a usual no-no for effective community bridge events), the funds raised were for a beloved local charity, and members of that charity were partners in the event. Hence, it worked in the church's favor in that community. There were activities, such as face painting for the kids. Complimentary refreshments were served to help provide opportunities for relationship building. It was a solid event with opportunities built-in to nurture relational connections with guests and use them to offer Jesus. Over time, decisions were made that, bit-by-bit, took the event off track and into the wilderness. The carnival atmosphere gradually disappeared. The "true north" moved gradually from making neighborhood connections to making money.

During a budget crunch, the funding

maintained the church's budget instead of
assisting a beloved local charity. Meanwhile,
the church was not known as a place where
disciples were made or a church that loved
building relationships in the community.
Instead, it was "that pumpkin patch church,"
known only as the place on the corner that
annually had a bunch of mostly unsold
pumpkins on its lawn. If you wanted a
pumpkin, you could purchase via the honor
system: just slide cash or check through the
mail slot in the door.

Did they still have a pumpkin patch? Well,
yes, so the annual task was completed! Did it
fulfill the mission or God-sized goals of the
church? Of course not! And by the end, it would
take a lot more than a map and compass to
get to the heart of how far the ministry had
gone off course. A strong Leadership Board
shouldn't be arranging the pumpkin deliveries
or scheduling disciples to serve shifts at the
carnival. In this case, the Leadership Board's
job is to hold the pastor accountable as the
pastor holds the ministry team accountable.
The ministry team is responsible for keeping
the bridge event oriented toward making
disciples and building relationships, and the
pastor is responsible for holding every aspect

of the event's planning and implementation accountable to this bigger mission.

In addition to mission drift, the metaphor of orienteering also helps us identify another challenge of the church: staying on course by focusing on ministries. Congregations can create elaborate catalogs of ministries, classes, and opportunities. The "attractional" church growth model that was so popular in the 1980s and 1990s was built on these full program calendars.

But this approach had multiple downsides. First, the stuffed calendars joined with the rise of organized team sports and traveling teams, deprive church members opportunities to bond as families and neighbors. Second, it exhausted the volunteer pool of disciples. Third, the lack of intentionality undercut important church-wide processes like intentional discipleship pathways and leadership development.

As stewards of the church's resources, the Leadership Board can counter this "shotgun approach" to ministry and instead focus on doing fewer things with excellence and deeper impact. One church from my district went from being birthed as a new daughter church based on small groups to a regular worship of hundreds. It did not succumb to the "be everything for everybody" approach to ministry, and instead, the church uses a shared curriculum every season for all of its small groups. They similarly focus on only one, possibly two, outreach mission opportunities each quarter. Everything else gets a "no," not because it's a bad idea or otherwise problematic, but because the church committed itself to stay simple and user-friendly to new Christians who could not possibly navigate a college course catalog-sized listing of dozens of opportunities.

Of course, it is much easier to create a church with this commitment to ministry simplicity than to reform one. Still, recently I have seen even mainline megachurches attempt simplicity in crafting their vision and God-sized goals. One large church that hosts an annual leadership event even printed their four aspirational core values as a bullet list on cocktail napkins to get the (simple) point across. Having attended small congregations that use up half their bulletin's cover with a paragraphs-long mission and vision statements, I must say that I appreciate the move towards simplicity. Outside the church bubble, simplicity is prized, and making your church easier to access is a must in today's over-committed environment.

How are or can your church's goals support a new expedition? How are they holding the new expedition back?

When I was in scouting, I was the proud owner of a Swiss Army Knife. It had all sorts of gadgets: scissors, saw, toothpick, tweezers, can opener, bottle opener, leather punch, and, of course, a couple of knife blades. My version also had a wine bottle corkscrew, a tool less than useful for a pre-teen kid on a hike. I loved the knife, but I must be honest. The can opener was kind of a pain – I would usually get the can opener with actual gears on it if I wanted actually to open a can. The knife blades didn't lock in place, so it was sort of dangerous. A three-inch saw is not nearly as useful in real life as it was to my 12-year-old imagination. And to my scoutmaster's relief, I never took a wine bottle out on a hike, so that corkscrew was useless. As cool as it was to have over a dozen tools in my hand at once, together they were often less useful than tools made specifically for a task.

Churches that try too hard to be Swiss Army Knives usually discover that all those ministries and programs, jumbled together, are less than the sum of their parts. Complexity and a packed program calendar have been prized for so long. It will require much discipline and focus on the part of the Leadership Board to strive instead for simplicity and excellence. Instead of dozens of programs, focus only on the ministries that will nurture disciples to have a committed relationship with Jesus Christ and offer hands-on opportunities to transform lives and communities.

Double-down on discipleship. Focus on doing a few ministries with excellence instead of being the Swiss Army Knife of churches, doing dozens of ministries with mediocrity. That kind of stewardship over the resources and mission of the church can only happen when the board has the backbone to say "no" even to wonderful ideas, all in service to God's larger mission and the mission of the congregation.

When your new simplified accountable Leadership Board's responsibilities cover all the critical areas of governance that were formerly spread out among multiple committees, time management will become an issue. Along the journey of the Leadership Board's work over a year, you will make some decisions. Don't let a good decision go to waste. Some decisions need only to be made once and then converted from unique and isolated decisions into policies and more universal guiding principles.

There is no reason to keep making the same decisions again and again if they can be published as policies or operating guidelines. For instance, during the COVID pandemic crisis, some congregations in my district created clear systems and actions to be taken if a staff member or worship attender became exposed or ill. Once those policy decisions were made, the pastors and staff of those congregations were comfortable activating the plans on an as-needed basis. Other churches wanted to simply "inform the board" in cases of exposure or infections, leading them to painstakingly meet every time a situation arose. Over time, they became exhausted. Governing by policy saves time and emotional energy that can be better used for creativity.

Over time, your policies and guiding principles become the traffic guard rails for the church ministries, keeping the church on the road toward fulfilling its mission. Policies, such as those governing staff vacation time or how ushers safeguard the offering after the worship service, allow some standardization to proceed in ministry. Guiding principles are slightly different –- they outline the boundaries on authority and expectations of the leadership. Individual decisions by the board/council on every ministry are no longer required on every matter. Monthly presentation and reports certainly are not required. Instead, permission-giving guiding principles are provided that allow staff and lay leaders to make decisions easily with flexibility, without the board/council micromanaging every decision.

Guiding principles could include pre-approval for maintenance team or discipleship curriculum purchases up to a certain amount, say $200, with treasurer approval required for purchases from $200-$1000 and the entire Leadership Board required to approve expenses over $1000. Another example of a guiding principle is to require someone with a new ministry idea first to get two or three other people on board and draft a ministry plan that includes a budget and a narrative of how the ministry idea will help move the church toward its God-sized goals. The appendix to this resource outlines some more topics you may want to consider as you create guiding principles.

Whenever the Leadership Board does make a decision, it also needs to ask itself, "Should this be a new standing guiding principle so that no one has to wait on us to make a decision next time?" Policies and guiding principles can be created to allow permission-giving to new ministries while making sure innovations align with the church's direction and vision.

How are, or can your church's guiding principles support(ing) a new expedition? How are they holding the new expedition back?

CHAPTER SIX
Accountability
Shakedowns and "Belay On"

In rock climbing, your belay partner stands on solid ground, holding the safety rope to an anchor point while you scale the cliff or the climbing wall. Depending on the style of rock climbing (going up) or rappelling (coming down), the exact nature of the belay role changes, but the basic job is to be alert and hold the rope to catch your partner. I remember doing some rappelling with some friends in high school. Yes, my friends jumped off a cliff, so I did, too!

That afternoon we were set up for high-speed descents. While we may have been 16-17 years old with zero parental supervision, we stuck to the rules. I yelled out, "On Belay!"

My partner William answered, "Belay On!" and I jumped off the cliff.

My rope was newer and slower. My buddy's

rope had quite a few more hours on it, and it
ran slicker than I was expecting. We were using
his rope that day. I may have actually friction-
burned through a pair of leather gloves over
the next three seconds. William saw I was out
of control, pulled tight the belay, and caught
me in a bear hug when I reached the ledge, so
I wouldn't go further down the steep slope at
the bottom. A belay partner has your life in his
hands. It takes trust.

When I think about accountability,
ministry evaluation, and the board's work in
overseeing and stewarding the ministries, I
remember the role of the belay. A Leadership
Board that understands healthy accountability
is willing to evaluate the situation and the
larger landscape, intervene, redirect, and,
sometimes, just make certain everyone is
safe. Your governing board is responsible and
accountable to God for the mission of Jesus. If
your board isn't accountable to the mission,
no one will be. If the board abdicates its role,
ministries can quickly fall off a cliff. In the
accountable leadership model, the board is
responsible for making the purpose (Kingdom
Impact) clear, and then setting up the systems
and processes for all levels of the church to

plan for impact (including setting up clear goals and measurements), implement impactful ministries (based on those goals), and then have appropriate evaluation of each ministry's Kingdom impact (using – you guessed it! – the predefined goals). By practicing and exhibiting accountability, the Leadership Board builds trust amongst the staff, clergy, and ministry team leaders so that the important "belay" work of the board will be appreciated and well-received.

There are two reasons that church consultant Kay Kotan and I use the term "Simplified Accountable Structure" to describe what is often called the single-board model. First, congregations sometimes mistakenly think that "single-board" means there are no other teams, task forces, or groups in the church. We actually encourage a simplified governance model to unleash MORE teams for ministry. The second reason we use "Simplified Accountable Structure" is because the whole model falls apart without accountability. In *IMPACT!*, we wrote:

> *Assessment, evaluation, and reflection are critically important to a healthy governance model when practicing accountable leadership.*

We must become proficient with assessment at every level. The board is accountable to Christ for the church living its mission of making disciples. The pastor is accountable to the board for the church's annual goals and living into its vision of God's preferred future for how it uniquely makes disciples. The staff (paid and unpaid ministry leaders) are accountable to the pastor for the day-to-day ministry, with the pastor ensuring that the ministries are aligned with the church's annual goals. Constant and consistent evaluation at all levels is critical to enable the church to assess its fruitfulness and remain in alignment of its purpose/mission. Finally, the board needs to take time to reflect on ministries and their effectiveness. Accountability is not about blaming, but it's certainly about learning. An organization that never reflects on their work never learns or adapts. A word of warning: Evaluation and accountability are key, but please know that this is an incredibly difficult shift to live into because it will take persistence and patience, but it will be so worth the investment.[3]

While churches are mostly made up of unpaid disciples, that does not relieve

---

[3] Kay Kotan and Blake Bradford. *Impact! Reclaiming the Call of Lay Ministry.* Market Square Books: Knoxville. 2018.

laity from accountability. Every disciple is accountable to Jesus Christ, and corporately, as the body of Christ called the church, we are accountable to Christ's mission. In our culture, that means job descriptions, reviews, and evaluations must be built-in to our "volunteer" positions and our ministries. Accountability is not a "one and done" evaluation: it needs to be a culture. I created a simple chart to outline the cycle of accountable leadership.

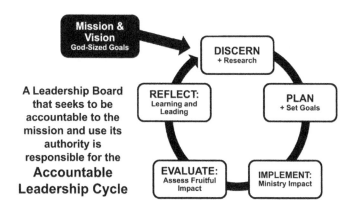

Accountable Leadership Cycle	
Mission, Vision, & Purpose (God-sized Goals)	Accountability is ultimately rooted in following the mission that Christ has for the congregation.
Discern + Research	The first step of the cycle is to discern ministry needs, as rooted in the mission. That not only takes prayerful conversation, but also research such as demographic studies, neighborhood prayer walks, community stakeholder interviews, and an assessment of a congregation's spiritual gifts and passions.
Plan + Set Ministry Goals	The Ministry Team should plan and set goals for the proposed ministry. For example, a "bridge event" to connect to neighbors will need plans for event staff to greet and get to know guests, not just "run the event." Similarly, a goal for such an event would be for appropriate guest follow-up within 24 hours. Ministries without planned goals for transformational impact become random "feel good events." The Ministry Team should connect with assigned staff or the pastor to ensure that clear goals are created and the ministry plans are designed to fulfill the goals.
Implement: Ministry Impact	The responsible ministry team is now ready to execute the plan. Ultimately, every serving disciple on the team is accountable to the mission of not only the particular ministry but to the congregation's larger overall mission and vision. Impactful ministries seek to make disciples and transform the world.
Evaluate: Assess Fruitful Impact	The Ministry Team should collaborate with the pastor or assigned staff/ministry team leader to assess the ministry from proposal to event to thank you notes. What worked well? What needed work? What surprised the team? Was there Kingdom impact? How did the ministry align with the stated goals? What did the team learn? Were there any Holy Spirit sightings during the ministry? This evaluation is a vital step in accountability.
Reflect: Learning and Leading	A solid evaluation allows the staff/ministry team leader and pastor to learn about the mission field and the congregation's ministry capacity. This reflection time is different from an evaluation. While an evaluation is about doing things right, reflection is about doing the right things. Reflection is a skill and an intentional practice that invites the congregation's leaders back into the season of prayerful discernment. The pastor will want to share their reflection learnings with the Leadership Board when it relates to the overall mission, vision, and church goals to identify any needed shifts required.

Adapted from Mission Possible 3+, page 124

In this model, the Leadership Board may not have a direct hand in every step of this cycle. Still, it is responsible for ensuring that the process cycle occurs by holding others to the appropriate level of accountability. Ministry implementation and the first set of evaluations may happen at a staff or ministry team level and reported to the pastor or the board. While the board will not be planning the ministry or the event themselves, they can, for example, be very clear about the goals of particular ministries. Likewise, it is the board that is ultimately responsible for engaging in reflection. For instance, the board's reflective work may include asking if a ministry fulfills the God-sized goals of the congregation or if these goals can be addressed by a different method and re-prioritize resources accordingly. In the previous example of the pumpkin patch, all the evaluations completed at the team level may say the event is a success if it made money. The board can push back by not being satisfied with that evaluation by referencing the real evangelism and relationship-building purposes of the pumpkin patch.

When I was a scout in the mid-1980s, a popular trip for the troop was going to Philmont Scout Ranch in New Mexico for

a multi-day backpacking adventure. When arriving, one of the first tasks, and well before starting out on the hike, was to unload all the backpacks and lay out every single item on the ground. This practice is called a "shakedown." In backpacking, ounces matter, and a solid shakedown means that only essential gear is taken on the journey. A few extra ounces add up to a few extra pounds of gear, which could mean a lot of pain and difficulty on the trail. Shakedowns were not designed to embarrass anyone and no scout was supposed to get bent out of shape when we removed some items from their bag. Everyone knew that a proper shakedown was needed to benefit the whole troop.

Churches are great at having backpacks full of ministries, events, and layered expectations. We scarcely have a new event without the title "First Annual" being attached. Over time, these ministries wax and wane in fruitfulness and participation. Mission field needs change, leaders arrive with different callings and ministry passions, and we start maintaining ministries more out of inertia and fear than mission and fruitfulness.

Our congregations need a ministry shakedown. When I served as a congregational coach and equipper for our regional denominational office, one of my gut-check tools (to see how serious a church's leadership was about missional fruitfulness) was to ask about the last few ministries that were shut down for ineffectiveness. It was common to get quizzical looks. Folks seem to think that ministries were granted eternal life, not disciples. But suppose we are really holding ministries accountable to our mission and vision. In that case, a certain number of these ministries will be ineffective and require a relaunch, a rethink, or a memorial service. "Well done, good and faithful ministry! You made an impact for Christ, and your season is now over." A proper ministry shakedown means there is more space left over in your church's backpack for new ministries that are relevant and impactful.

As congregations came out of COVID quarantines, I used my role as a district superintendent to recommend that leaders carefully and prayerfully consider relaunching every new ministry because the pandemic offered a clear "shakedown" opportunity. In my visits with leaders, I often used a metaphor from the kitchen: in their return to in-person ministries (often with fewer people available), some ministries needed to go in the oven to start cooking, some needed to go on the counter to be prepared for the new era, and some needed to go in the refrigerator or maybe even the deep freeze, to be pulled out only if circumstances were right. Every church has less than fruitful ministries, and now was an excellent time to lay those aside to leave more bandwidth for sustainability and creativity.

Evaluating ministries as an ongoing practice, along with regular ministry shakedowns, ensure that your congregation is ready and resourced to make disciples and transform your community and the world. Don't get stuck maintaining yesterday's ministries at the expense of God's calling today.

How would you rate your church's practice accountability and evaluation? How will those practices support or hold back a new expedition?

CHAPTER SEVEN
Fruitful Meetings Are About the Right Questions

While I may have been emphatic in starting this resource with the declaration that "meetings are not ministry," please don't take this to mean that meetings don't matter. Gathering in person or online for meetings is crucial. Fruitful meetings are our vehicle for decision-making and solid Christ-centered governance. Group conversation, discernment, and decision-making is like tending a garden.

Gardening takes great seeds, weeding, tending the soil with water and nutrients, and ensuring ample sunlight. Luke 8 shares Jesus' parable of the sower and how the Word of God can produce a hundredfold harvest in the right earth. Similarly, meetings require care and good gardening if you expect them to be fruitful.

The Seeds

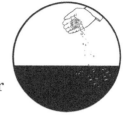

Let's start with the seeds: as a fan of resources provided by the Lewis Center for Church Leadership at Wesley Theological Seminary, I know well the admonition from Lovett Weems: "Leaders do not need answers. Leaders must have the right questions." While this will take one only so far (after all, answers are eventually needed), the statement does reframe the work of leadership. The pastor or the board chair shouldn't be expected to come to every meeting with a set of answers, ready to unload them at the meeting. Why would you need a board then? Instead, by asking critical questions, the leader can sow seeds of innovation and discernment amongst the board, with the team then formulating the prayerful answers and decisions that can take your congregation toward fulfilling the church's mission.

The first seeds needed for a meeting come in the preparation for the meeting. I have attended too many meetings where, when I showed up, there were 10 stacks of documents, and the leader said, "that's our agenda and everything for the meeting; pick up one of each before you get seated." In that stack , I might find the monthly financials, some reports, maybe a set of bids for a remodeling project, and a new multi-page policy that I quickly try to scan before the meetin's opening prayer. Then, after the meeting commenced, we spent our time reading through a stack of documents that should have arrived in everyone's email inbox a week ago. Without a prepared leadership packet, we waste precious meeting time trying to play catch up, and our discussion becomes reckless and uneven. So, send your seeds out early! Send a leadership packet with the agenda and all the "handouts" needed for the meeting. Many matters then can be summarily approved using the parliamentary "consent calendar" process, which approves all requests not pulled by the board for more discussion.

The right questions are the seeds that build up the capacity of the entire congregation to lead. In a March 19, 2005, article in the *Harvard Business Review* titled "How to Design an Agenda for an Effective Meeting," Roger Schwarz offered an excellent tool for building meeting agendas based entirely on the concept of asking the right questions. The article provides several best practices, but here are a few critical suggestions:

- First, he recommends leaders collaborate early and ask the team to contribute items and questions that reflect their needs to be engaged in the meeting. I've attended too many meetings in which I was a superfluous attendee and not a participant because the agenda only reflected the leader's needs and not the entire group's needs. Further, Schwarz suggests that if the chair doesn't include a requested item, the chair should show accountability to the team member by explaining why it was excluded. It actually might be a teachable moment in that the requested topic is not yet ripe for discussion, maybe it doesn't fit the steering role of the group, perhaps permission already exists in guiding principles, or the topic is not relevant to the entire board and needs to be handled offline. By explaining why you exclude a request, you are not only showing respect for the board member but helping equip the team for a higher functioning leadership.

- The next helpful practice that Roger Schwarz uses is to convert agenda topics into action-oriented questions and include a designation of whether the purpose of the agenda item is to simply update folks with information (which I would suggest belongs in a written report, if possible), seek the group's input for a leader to make a decision, or if the group is being asked to make a decision or approve an action itself. Here is the problem that Schwarz is trying to solve: imagine an agenda item that simply says "Fall Festival." Just looking at the agenda, some people might be coming to the meeting to argue whether the church can afford it this year, other board members may be wanting to do an evaluation, others thinking a theme is being selected, one is already ordering the pumpkins, and some board members come with suggestions about relocating it to a downtown park location and converting into an evangelism opportunity instead of an insider event. By writing the item as a question, such as "How can we ensure that the Fall Festival is designed to be a Community Bridge Event to connect with potential guests?" you are setting expectations for the agenda item. Creating the right question also lets Leadership Board members know what is expected of them in the meeting. Schwarz writes, "It's difficult for team members to participate effectively if they don't know whether to simply listen, give their input, or be part of the decision-making process. If people think they are involved in making a decision, but you simply want their input, everyone is likely to feel frustrated by the end of the conversation." By writing agenda items as questions, you also empower the entire team to help keep the meeting succinct and on track. Board members can police each other by referring to the agenda question when the topic strays from the question at hand.

Both of these suggestions take an approach to leadership that is collaborative, and I see this approach as lifting up the power of "the right questions."

You will note in this meeting model that there is no time set aside for reporting. That is intentional! All reports (including financials) should be sent out in writing a week before the meeting so that precious meeting time is not used up by endless reports of past events that would be better shared in an email. By starting with the seeds of excellent questions, even in your agenda creation, you are focusing on the power of the Leadership Board's gathered wisdom.

Weeding

Despite my Arkansas upbringing, I am what most Arkansans would consider a city boy as I have little experience in agriculture. I do, however, know about weeds. While a solid agenda may plant the right seeds, a group is always in danger of heading off into the weeds, either by going off-topic or wasting valuable time. Gardening is a constant battle with weeds that threaten to pull resources from the plants or even overwhelm them by crowding out and smothering what we are trying to grow. As we apply the gardening metaphor to meetings, I think of the weeding task as leading meetings in a way that creates optimal focus on the actual work of the board's governance and decision-making work. Here are some recommendations as you do weeding for your meetings:

- **Practice mutual accountability from the beginning.** We are accountable first to Jesus Christ and God's mission for us as a church. If the Leadership Board isn't accountable, then no one will be.

- **Encourage leaders to come with a sense of curiosity and grace.** Members shouldn't be afraid to ask questions. Outside agendas need to be left at the door. These meetings are God's time.

- **Configure your space to have meaningful conversation.** Gather in a circle so you can see each other. Have team members sit at the table and observers sit in chairs along the wall to define those with voting rights clearly. Perhaps light a candle in the center representing Jesus at the table. I once attended an administrative council meeting at a church I was coaching where all the board members were seated up front in a row, and the "audience" were in rows in front of them. It reminded me of a City Council or School Board meeting where constituents could go up to the microphone to argue their point to the board. Meanwhile, the board members couldn't even see each other. The space and configuration dictated an "us/ them" approach to everything the board did.

- **Use Guiding Principles to reduce the number of decisions the Board needs to make.** Every time a decision is made, ask if it needs to become a church policy or a new Guiding Principle. A sample of topics to create your own Guiding Principles is in the appendix. After you build your initial set, remember that Guiding Principles are a living, breathing document that are open to edits and additions as needed to provide permission-giving ministry within healthy boundaries.

- **Create a time docket for your meetings.** One of the recommendations in Roger Schwarz's *HBR* article, "How to Design an Agenda for an Effective Meeting," is to post a time window for every agenda item. This practice of allocating time to each item requires the chair to be realistic with the time available and to calculate how much time can be given to each item. With a 9-person board plus the pastor, if everyone is expected to speak for a minute to share their opinion, there are 10 minutes used on an item. If you give an item 5 minutes, you are expecting no comments. Schwarz shares that when you have an agenda with printed times, board members can then adjust their comments to fit the time allotted, they can suggest that the item be picked up in a future called meeting, or maybe a small offline team needs to work up a proposal for the entire board to act upon. I have used a time docket for years, and it helps the chair create expectations for the team. Of course, the group can always adjust as needed, but without any printed time allocation, team members can quickly get frustrated or feel like the chair is railroading the meeting. Notice that in both the matter of the time docket and the use of printed agenda questions with action designations, I am attempting to harness the entire team in being gardening partners in the weeding. By setting up clear expectations, the chair can rely on the board to self-regulate.

- **Creating clear processes for addressing agenda items.** There are times when your board will need to take votes. Consensus is a fine enough goal, and it is lovely when the board is all in agreement, but consensus cannot be a requirement for your church to move forward. After a few decades, I still vividly remember a classroom exercise during the seminary leadership course; we were all given a role to play and told our hypothetical church would be given a large financial gift. Then, we were set free to figure out what to do with the large bequest. It was a mess. Some wanted to vote. The assigned chairperson wanted a unanimous consensus to move forward (a process she declared without input). Even with a bunch of seminarians playing with monopoly money, we spent over an hour with nothing to show of it but bruised feelings. Since then, I have seen churches who utilize a unanimous consent requirement become immobilized by a minority of members who held the church's future hostage. In the *HBR* article by Schwarz, he recommends:

> *Propose a process for addressing each agenda item... Agreeing on a process significantly increases meeting effectiveness, yet leaders rarely do it. Unless the team has agreed on a process, members will, in good faith, participate based on their own process. You've probably seen this in action: some team members are trying to*

*define the problem, other team members
are wondering why the topic is on the
agenda, and still other members are already
identifying and evaluating solutions. When
you reach that item during the meeting,
explain the process and seek agreement:
"I suggest we use the following process.
First, let's take about 10 minutes to get
all the relevant information on the table.
Second, let's take another 10 minutes to
identify and agree on any assumptions we
need to make. Third, we'll take another
10 minutes to identify and agree on the
interests that should be met for any solution.
Finally, we'll use about 15 minutes to craft
a solution that ideally takes into account
all the interests, and is consistent with our
relevant information and assumptions. Any
suggestions for improving this process?"*

**"How to Design an Agenda for an Effective Meeting," by
Roger Schwarz, *Harvard Business Review*, March 19, 2005**

Notice in his recommendation that the chair
isn't expected to have a single decision-making
process and stick to it rigidly for every item and
topic. Instead, the process can be customized as
needed depending on the matter at hand. For
instance, I was trained early in my ministry
on the "6 Thinking Hats System" created
by business consultant Edward de Bono.
I especially love it for brainstorming and

innovation work. However, there are plenty of situations where other techniques are more valuable. I have a whole other toolbox for conflict transformation that involves listening sessions. I have had tense meetings as a denominational official that required Robert's Rules of Order because the congregation simply didn't have the creative bandwidth for anything else. However, the point of this recommendation is not to use a particular system but to be clear about the system the group will be using and have buy-in *before* getting to the question at hand.

All these recommendations are about tending to the garden, that is, the team members' relationships and emotions during the meeting so that the decision-making work of the board can be appropriately addressed without getting "stuck in the weeds."

Tending the Soil

For church leadership teams, I believe that tending the soil adds the healthy nutrients a team needs, such as spiritual formation and leadership equipping. In the Arkansas Conference Cabinet, we use an L3 model of

"Love, Learn, Lead," with every meeting starting with rotating leadership sharing devotional and prayer, followed by a section devoted to learning about leadership in today's world. After these components, we move on toward "lead" – the agenda-based work of governance and making decisions.

I worked with a church that never thought they needed these components, and it showed. One leader told me, "We already did church today. Just say a prayer, and let's move on."

NO! If we lose Jesus Christ as the foundation of our being and his Great Commission as our mission, I believe that we will cease to be the disciples God is calling us to be. If we simply plow through our agenda without connecting to the Holy Spirit, our leaders will start putting our wants, desires, and opinions ahead of our Christian mission. Our meetings need some watering from the Wellspring of Life that is Jesus.

And as for leadership equipping, I don't care how "successful" a congregation has been in its past; there is no way past effectiveness guarantees future fruitfulness. The world is moving too quickly for those assumptions, so we must always be a learning community

of leaders. Additionally, I would hope the
new disciples are always being added to the
Leadership Board. Their fresh eyes are part of
the new soil that the board needs and they will
need equipping on congregational leadership.

Sunlight

One of the challenges
of a simplified accountable
leadership structure is that it
dramatically reduces the number
of leaders in positions to know what is going
on in a congregation. Suppose the church had
five administrative committees, and those
responsibilities become condensed into a
single Leadership Board. In that case, you
need to communicate five times as much just to
maintain your current level of communication.
There is also a team-building process that
grows with a board that can become isolating.
The spiritual formation work and leadership
development that the pastor and board do
together at the meeting table can easily distance
the board from the conversations congregants
are having. Unless carefully tended, the board
begins to operate within its reality.

Supreme Court Justice Louis Brandeis

wrote that "sunlight is said to be the best of disinfectants" in a 1913 *Harper's Weekly* article entitled "What Publicity Can Do." The work of the Leadership Board needs sunlight for our own accountability to God's mission and to maintain the integrity and trust that is required of spiritual leaders. I believe that every church meeting should be considered an open meeting except for very defined situations, such as staffing matters and legal negotiations (such as the sale of property). By being relentlessly transparent in matters of church leadership in the majority of issues, the congregation will come to respect your team in matters that must be confidential.

Sunshine can also shine forth from regular "Town Hall Meetings," "Quarterly Conferences," or "State of the Church" online or in-person meetings. Choose a name that is appropriate and appealing in your context. The important thing here is not in the title of the gathering but in its practice. In *Mission Possible*, we suggested holding these quarterly as you transition into the simplified, accountable structure. As time goes by and the congregation becomes more comfortable with the model, the conversation frequency may need to be only a couple of times per year. The gathering is led by the board chair or a designated leader who is gifted in communications. To support and encourage the ministry of the laity, the pastor is in attendance but does not lead the conversation. The purpose of the conversation is to build trust through transparency, continuously cast the vision, offer information to the congregation, receive feedback, and answer questions. Most congregational communication strategies are one-way. Town halls and other congregational feedback opportunities provide the possibility of two-way conversations, which are vital. People need to be heard, and they need to know that the board is listening.

Design these meetings with care to encourage conversations and not airing grievances from a microphone pointed at the board. In larger settings, use table groups to help folks feel comfortable sharing and to reduce the chance of a member hijacking the meeting. Notice, I do not say that these gatherings include taking votes on matters. They are about relationships, trust, and communications, not voting. Taking votes in these gatherings will soon destroy the accountability that the board will need to truly govern.

In addition to open meetings and regular town halls designed for two-way communications, I also have begun to recommend that every board conclude each meeting with a communications conversation. The question that should end every meeting is, "What does the congregation need to know from today's meeting, and how shall it be communicated?" Maybe a decision needs to be shared in an email blast written by the chair or included in a congregation meeting, or a video of the pastor on social media. By closing each meeting with a communications agenda item, you ensure that the work of the board gets sunshine and that the work of the board doesn't become detached from the life of the congregation.

Trailhead

When I went hiking as a Boy Scout, the trailhead indicated the start of the journey and also the end of a hike. It all depended on which way we were going. In the Arkansas State Parks that I grew up exploring, several trailheads have signs that face both ways as a reminder for those beginning or ending their hike for the day. The signs offered the pithy aphorism: "Take nothing but pictures. Leave nothing but footprints." That is a great representation of "low impact" camping and enjoyment of the outdoors. Of course, my hope and prayer for you is just the opposite: as Christians, we are called and sent by Jesus to make a God-sized impact in lives, neighborhoods, communities, and even the world. So, gather your Expedition Team, grab your map, pack the tools and resources you will need, and let's start the adventure of being a fruitful, faithful Church of Jesus Christ!

Expedition Outfitters: Supplies for the Journey

A stop by the wilderness outfitter is essential before you begin your journey. This appendix includes some lists and samples that will assist you in your expedition.

- Sample Nominations list

- Potential Guiding Principles

- Sample Monthly Board Agenda

Sample Nominations Officiary Report

2023 Anytown First UMC Leadership
(Adapted from Resource 8 of Mission Possible 3+)

- Anytown United Methodist Church is governed according to the denomination's prescribed structure as found in *The United Methodist Book of Discipline.* All *Book of Discipline* and congregational policy references to the Church Council, Board of Trustees, Staff/Pastor Parish Relations Committee, Endowment Committee, and Finance Committee shall be understood to refer to the Leadership Board. Where years are listed, they represent the final year of an individual's term.

- The Nominations Committee has undertaken a careful and discerning process of preparing the slate below for approval by the Church Conference. The committee's aim is to match persons with open positions according to the following considerations:

  ¤ Maturity as a Disciple of Jesus Christ

  ¤ Alignment with the church's mission: "Making Disciples of Jesus Christ for the Transformation of the world"

  ¤ Length of membership tenure at Anytown UMC, with a balancing of experience in leadership with welcoming and engaging new leaders

  ¤ Actively fulfilling member expectations (UM Discipline ¶217): prayers, presence, gifts, service, and witness

- ¤ History of leadership in small groups, classes, ministry teams, and committees

- ¤ Balance and diversity of the committee, particularly with age, gender, and areas of involvement

- ¤ Ability to fulfill board requirements, the Board Covenant, and actively participate in meetings.

- As part of our Intentional Leadership Pathway, In *YEAR*, a class of "Preparatory Members" was created who will serve one year with voice, but without vote to prepare those who may subsequently be elected to serve a three-year voting term. In the event of a vacancy, the preparatory may be asked to complete a term.

Anytown FUMC Charge Conference

- The Charge Conference includes the members of the Leadership Board, the Nominations Committee, pastors appointed to the congregation, and all active and retired clergy who have designated our congregation as their home Charge Conference.

- To "encourage broader participation by members of the church, the nominations committee recommends that Anytown FUMC request that any annual or called Charge Conference be convened as a Church Conference to extend the vote to all professing members of the congregation (2016 *Book of Discipline of The United Methodist Church,* ¶248).

- The Leadership Board serves as the incorporated institution's board of directors and serves as the executive committee of the Charge Conference.

Leadership Board

Version with ELEVEN voting on the Board

(Includes separate Lay Leader and Lay Member of AC who are not disciplinarily term-limited)

Class of 2023

John Jones, T/F/SPR
Yolanda Youngperson, F/SPR/Y
Mary Miller, T/F/SPR

Class of 2024

Jennifer Jackson, T/F/SPR/C
Larry Lewis, T/F/SPR
Ron Roberts, T/F/SPR/Treasurer

Class of 2025

Sue Smith, T/F/SPR/UMW
David Dent, T/F/SPR/UMM
Debbie Duncan, T/F/SPR

Preparatory Member

Andrea Anderson (non-voting)

Ex-Officio Members:

Lay Leader: Ben Black, F/SPR/LL
Lay Member of AC: Carol Clark, F/SPR/LM

Key

- **T** – Trustee (min 3 and max 9, and includes at least 1/3 men and at least 1/3 women)

- **SPRC** – Staff Parish Relations Committee, (min 5 and max 9, not including the Lay Leader and Lay Member to Annual Conference who are members)

- **F** – Finance

- **LM** – Lay Member to Annual Conference (Ex Officio on SPRC)

- **LL** – Lay Leader (Ex Officio on SPRC)

- **C** – Chair

- **UMM** – United Methodist Men

- **UMW** – United Methodist Women

- **Y** – Youth (Note: members under 18 cannot be elected Trustee)

Notes:

- At the January meeting, Leadership Board will elect a Trustee Chairperson, which may be the Leadership Board Chairperson.

- Leadership Board may assign team members as Primary Contacts for matters pertaining to building maintenance, personnel, financial matters, or other areas of responsibility. Still, the Leadership Board operates as a single body encompassing the responsibilities of SPRC, Finance Committee, Endowment Committee, and Trustees.

Nominations Committee

Chairperson is the Appointed Senior Pastor (max nine members, not including the pastor)

Class of 2023	Class of 2024	Class of 2025
Carl Clark	Rollie Rich	Sally Smith
Belle Brady	Gene Galloway	Rob Roberts

Potential Topics for Guiding Principles

(Adapted from Resource 12 of Mission Possible 3+)

Potential Topics for Guiding Principle Consideration

- Mission, vision, core values of the church

- Identification of the board's role, powers, responsibilities, and authority in regards to the denomination's polity

- The Board will ensure there is a current organizational chart reflective of the current decision-making process and chain of command at all times.

- The Board is to provide transparent and routine communication to keep the congregation informed of missional effectiveness and resource alignment.

- Financial and credit card expenditure approval rules and limits for staff, the pastor, and the building maintenance team

- Hiring/terminating authority of the pastor and other paid staff

- References to church-wide policies:

  ¤ Building and equipment usage policies (for example, rental policies for members, internal ministry groups, outside non-profit groups, or for-profit businesses)

  ¤ Safe sanctuary policies for child protection, sexual harassment, and sexual misconduct

  ¤ Employee handbook

- ¤ Building safety

- ¤ Technology usage and safety

- ¤ Counters' policies and procedures

- Parliamentary rules of order, such as the usage of Robert's Rules of Order, the consensus method, or other variations.

- How to change a guiding principle

- Expectations for those wanting approval to create a new Church-sponsored ministry

- Role and function of the building maintenance team

- Authority and responsibility of the treasurer

- Relationship of Nominations and Lay Leadership Development to the Leadership Board

- Boundaries that state how individual board members may make (or not) demands on staff time outside formal board requests

- How daycare and/or preschool relate to the church, pastor, and leadership board *(There is a huge legal and governance difference between childcare ministries that operate under a church's ministry and childcare ministries that exist as a separate but related 501(c)(3) – these differences will impact how your write your guiding principle defining the relationship.)*

- Defining public meetings vs. executive session (such as personnel matters when the board is operating as the congregation's personnel committee, or S/PPRC)

- Official record-keeping and access to records of meetings and executive session minutes.

Guiding Principles Examples

The following guiding principles are offered to you as guidelines or thought-starters. These are not intended to be a complete set of building principles. In fact, you will find a few of the guiding principles are contradictory to one another. This is intentional and is offered to remind churches of the importance of clarity around specific principles. Guiding principles are intended to be a permission-giving tool to eliminate waiting on decisions or permission as a bottle-neck to ministry flow. Guiding principles provide healthy boundaries and macro rather than micro decision-making, and should be living documents, edited and updated to encourage impactful ministry and healthy accountability. Every church has its own unique setting, so special care and attention in this work will prove to pay dividends for years to come.

- All references to the Church Council, Board of Trustees, Staff/Pastor Parish Relations Committee, Endowment Committee, and Finance Committee, in all congregational policies as of _____ , and in all references in the Book of Discipline of the United Methodist *Church,* shall be understood to refer to the Leadership Board beginning _____ .

- The pastor is responsible for reviewing line items within ministry areas with the appropriate staff or team leaders for accountability from the staff and to the board. The pastor(or designated supervisor) is responsible for reviewing line items within ministry areas with the appropriate staff or team leaders for accountability from the staff and to the board. The ministry team leader or staff member responsible for the purchase will provide documentation of the bids to the leadership board for purposes of accountability and documentation*

- Once the budget is approved, those responsible (i.e. staff and team leaders) for the various ministry areas have the authority to spend their ministry budget to align with the objectives for their ministry area approved by the pastor. No further approval is needed to access the budget in their area of responsibility, except as indicated in other guiding principles.*

- Any member of the Building Maintenance Team has the authority to purchase supplies for building maintenance and improvement up to $_____ without approval. The Building Maintenance Team leader can authorize purchases for building maintenance and improvement up to $_____ . Purchases up to $_____ can be approved by the pastor (executive pastor or business manager). Any purchases over $_____ need Leadership Board approval unless the expenditure is already approved in a capital expenditure line item in the approved budget, except as indicated in other guiding principles *

- Any expenditure over $_____ will require

three bids. Preference will be given to hire local companies offering competitive bids within __% of other bids. If the expenditure is already approved in the budget, there is no further approval needed, except as indicated in other guiding principles.* The pastor is responsible for reviewing line items within ministry areas with the appropriate staff or team leaders for accountability from the staff and to the board. The ministry team leader or staff member responsible for the purchase will provide documentation of the bids to the leadership board for purposes of accountability and documentation*

- *The treasurer must be consulted concerning any single purchase or expenditure over $_____ for purposes of cash flow. The treasurer does not approve or deny purchases but rather confirms large purchases will not create cash flow issues.

- The pastor has the authority to hire and release employees using the church's employee policies and procedures in the _____ UMC Employee Handbook. When terminating an employee, the pastor will invite a board member to sit in on the exit conversation for purposes of liability protection. The pastor has the responsibility to supervise, discipline, and evaluate staff performance as outlined in the _____ UMC Employee Handbook.

- The authority to hire and terminate employees of the church shall be vested in the Leadership Board. The pastor shall have the authority to interview and recommend candidates to fill open staff positions. The Board shall have the sole authority to determine the number of staff positions, approve job descriptions for each staff member and set the salary paid to each staff member. The Leadership Board delegates to the pastor the authority to supervise, discipline, and manage paid staff.

- The pastor will review all paid staff annually using the approval evaluation process in the employee manual dated _____. Paid staff will review unpaid staff/team and leaders annually using the same evaluation process.

- The Weekday Child Care Advisory Board (BOD Paragraph 256.2.c) is fully amenable and accountable to the Leadership Board, and shall submit an annual budget and recommended policy changes to the Leadership Board. The director of weekday ministries is supervised by the pastor.

- The board recognizes and approves the Building Usage Policies dated _____.

- The board recognizes and approves the Building Security and Key Policies dated _____.

- The board recognizes and approves the Financial Controls Policies dated _____.

- The board recognizes and approves the _____ UMC Personnel Policies date _____.

- All meetings of the Leadership Board shall be open to the public, with the exception of any meeting or portion of a meeting in which a personnel matter or a matter of legal negotiations is considered. In those cases, the Board will transition into executive session. Minutes of executive session agenda items concerning personnel matters will be kept separately as part of the "S/PPRC" files.

- Leadership Board members are nominated by a separate and independent Nominations and Lay Leadership Development Committee, chaired by the pastor, and elected by the Charge Conference as described in the BOD. The Nominations Committee will be responsible for developing new leaders and equipping them for future leadership board positions.

- Due to the Leadership Board's serving as the congregation's Staff-Parish Relations Committee, no immediate family member of the pastor or other paid staff person may serve as a member of the board. Due to serving as the congregation's Board of Trustees, only Leadership Board members over the age 18 will have voting privileges in matters of property, incorporation, legal matters, contracts, insurance, investments, or other matters described in the BOD paragraphs 2525-2551.

- The Lead Pastor is the Leadership Board's link to church ministry and programming. The Lead Pastor has complete authority and accountability for all staffing, including hiring, evaluating, firing, and consideration of raises. The Board will never give instructions to persons who report directly or indirectly to the Lead Pastor.

- Compensation for the Lead Pastor and all appointed clergy will be determined by a Charge/Church Conference. Recommendations for the clergy compensation will be made by the Leadership Board (as part of their SPRC duties) for consideration before the Charge/Church Conference.

- The Lead Pastor shall not cause or allow any activity, decision, or organizational circumstance that is unlawful or in violation of commonly accepted business practices and professional ethics. Furthermore, the Lead Pastor shall not cause or allow any activity, decision, or organizational circumstance that is a violation of the current Book of Discipline, Standing Rules of the Annual Conference, or the express direction of the Resident Bishop and/or District Superintendent of The Annual Conference.

Sample Monthly Board Agenda

(Adapted from Resource 13 of Mission Possible 3+)

AnyTown Church
Leadership Team Meeting

Our Mission: To make new disciples of Jesus Christ for the transformation of the world.

Our Vision: Each of us at AnyTown Church is on a journey to grow closer to God, to be more like Jesus, and to be filled with the Holy Spirit. No matter where you are in your walk with Christ, you are invited to journey and grow with us through the power of the Holy Spirit, so that we can fulfill God's commission.

Core Values: Excellence, evangelism, engagement, equipping, expansion and encouragement.

6:00pm	Opening Prayer:	Jennifer Jackson, Chair
6:00pm	Spiritual Formation:	David Dent
6:15pm	Leadership Equipping:	Carol Clark
6:25pm	Review of New People:	Pastor Taylor
6:30pm	Goal Review and Accountability Conversation:	Pastor Taylor
6:50pm	Packet and Consent Calendar Items	

6:55pm   Questions   Jennifer Jackson
          6:55: Question #1
          7:15: Question #2
          7:35: Question #3

7:55pm   Communication: What needs to be shared and
          how to share it?

8:00pm   Closing Prayer: Debbie Duncan

Next Meeting is (date) _____

About the Author

Rev. Blake Bradford is the Distcit Superintendent in the Arkansas Conference of The United Methodist Church and Dean of the Appointive Cabinet. A co-author of the books, *IMPACT! Reclaiming the Call of Lay Ministry* and *Mission Possible 3+: A Simple Structure for Missional Effectiveness*, Blake is a graduate of Hendrix College, with master's degrees from Vanderbilt University and Iliff School of Theology, and a Doctor of Ministry degree from Perkins School of Theology at SMU.

Over 20 years of ministry, Blake has pastored churches of different sizes and contexts. His most recent parish appointment has been as executive pastor of St. James United Methodist Church in Little Rock. In this 3500-member congregation, he worked with clergy, staff, and lay leadership to align and coordinate the church's ministries. Dr. Bradford directed the ordination curriculum for the Arkansas Conference Board of Ordained Ministry for over a decade as a member of its executive committee, assisted the bishop as the Annual Conference Parliamentarian, and teaches pastoral leadership, polity, and administration for the Course of Study School.

Before his appointment to the Cabinet, he served the Arkansas Conference Center for Vitality as a congregational coach, consultant, and conflict transformation mediator. A speaker across the country, Blake has offered a keynote at the General Board of Higher Education and Ministry's Quadrennial Training for Boards of Ordained Ministry and led workshops at the Church of the Resurrection's Leadership Institute.

Blake and his wife Kerri are from Little Rock, Arkansas, and have two children, Bailey and Micah. Blake also holds a second-degree black belt, which he believes may have been his best training for ministry!

Learn more and download resources at:
www.blakebradford.org.

Learn More about Simplified, Accountable Leadership Structure

This expedition resource is a primer on rethinking your leadership structures to support new expeditions. The "owner's manual" of simplified accountable leadership structures is *Mission Possible: A Simple Structure for Missional Effectiveness*, a resource from Market Square Books by Kay Kotan and Blake Bradford.

In *Mission Possible*, Kay and Blake focus on ministry while making meetings fewer in number but larger in meaning. In this book aimed at congregational leaders, particularly United Methodists, the authors provide practical, field-tested steps to simplify your church structure and unleash more people into ministry.

Too often, churches try to simplify their structures by just having fewer people at the meeting table. But real simplicity and accountable leadership mean that meetings – and leaders – are transformed. Kay and Blake walk you through the technical and adaptive changes to simplify your structure for missional effectiveness.

About the Authors

Kay Kotan is a professionally credentialed coach who has coached hundreds of pastors and churches across the nation, helping them become more vital in reaching new people. She has authored more than a dozen books on church and leadership transformation. Kotan was the primary creator of the Small Church Initiative under the HCI process.

Blake Bradford is a United Methodist minister appointed as a mission strategist and district superintendent in the Arkansas Conference. He has pastored churches of different sizes and contexts and has served the conference's Center for Vitality as a congregational coach, consultant, and director of the ordination program.

WWW.MARKETSQUAREBOOKS.COM

Learn More about Developing Lay Leaders

This expedition resource is a primer on rethinking your leadership structures to support new expeditions. Strong leadership structures depend on strong lay leaders. *Impact!: Reclaiming the Call of Lay Ministry,* a resource from Market Square Books by Kay Kotan and Blake Bradford, is designed to support, encourage, and develop disciples to grow in their congregational leadership.

Every Christian is called to ministry. Help the people of your congregation claim their call!

The ancient church spread rapidly throughout the Mediterranean world. Centuries later, the Methodist Church spread like wildfire on the American frontier thanks largely to lay Christians who shared the Christian faith in their homes and communities. Over time, our primary church leadership models have emphasized the leadership of the clergy and have devalued the ministry of the laity. *IMPACT* offers practical and proven plans to help clergy and laity partner together again to spread the Gospel in a new day and age!

About the Authors

Kay Kotan is a professionally credentialed coach who has coached hundreds of pastors and churches across the nation, helping them become more vital in reaching new people. She has authored more than a dozen books on church and leadership transformation. Kotan was the primary creator of the Small Church Initiative under the HCI process.

Blake Bradford is a United Methodist minister appointed as a mission strategist and district superintendent in the Arkansas Conference. He has pastored churches of different sizes and contexts and has served the conference's Center for Vitality as a congregational coach, consultant, and director of the ordination program.

WWW.MARKETSQUAREBOOKS.COM

Quotes From Other Books
in The Greatest Expedition Series

The multi-site movement keeps the church centered on God's consistent call to go and make disciples for the transformation of the world while staying connected to one another in community.

Ken Nash
Multi-Site Ministry

Stay flexible even when it is not easy. Due to the stress and responsibility of ministry, we can become rigid, pessimistic and fail to see the opportunities in front of us. A mark of great leadership is flexibility, being able to make adjustments when necessary.

Olu Brown
New Kind of Venture Leader

But let me be clear, we will not be making the case that online relationships and connections are the same as in-person ones; we all know they are not. But we will be talking about why online connections are valuable, and there is nothing "virtual" or "almost" about them.

Nicole Reilley
Digital Ministry

Quotes From Other Books
in The Greatest Expedition Series

While we find struggling churches in different contexts, theological backgrounds, sizes, and cultures, declining congregations have one thing in common: There is a palpable lack of focus on what God desires.

Jaye Johnson
Missional Accountability

How you think of your church will determine not only your priorities, but also your energy investment and actions. It will define how you lead and to what extent you live into what the church of Jesus Christ is intended to be.

Sue Nilson Kibbey
Open Road

Any collaboration with local people is a good thing – but the best collaboration is spiritual. It is where we begin to pray together about the community, and the emerging ministry. In such a spiritual collaboration, amazing things begin to happen.

Paul Nixon
Cultural Competency

What is *The Greatest Expedition*?

The Greatest Expedition is a congregational journey for churches, charges, or cooperative parishes led by a church Expedition Team of 8-12 brave pioneering leaders. The purpose of *The Greatest Expedition* is to provide an experience for Expedition Teams to explore their local context in new ways to develop new MAPS (ministry action plans) so you are more relevant and contextual to reach new people in your community. Updated tools and guides are provided for the church's Expedition Team. Yet, it is a "choose your own adventure" type of journey.

The tools and guides will be provided, but it is up to the church's Expedition Team to decide which tools are needed, which tools just need sharpening, which tools can stay in their backpack to use at a later time, what pathways to explore, and what pathways to pass.

the greatest
EXPEDITION

The Greatest Expedition provides a new lens and updated tools to help your Expedition Team explore and think about being the church in different ways. Will your Expedition Team need to clear the overgrown brush from a once known trail, but not recently traveled? Or will the Expedition Team need to cut a brand new trail with their new tools? Or perhaps, will the Team decide they need to move to a completely fresh terrain and begin breaking ground for something brand new in a foreign climate?

Registration is open and Expedition Teams are launching!

greatestexpedition.com

the greatest
EXPEDITION

the greatest
EXPEDITION

A New Kind
of

**Venture
Leader**

Olu Brown

EXPANDING
THE
EXPEDITION
THROUGH

**Digital
Ministry**

Nicole Reilley

the greatest
EXPEDITION

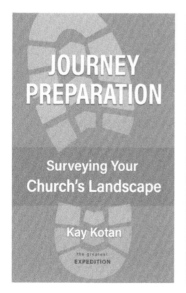

**JOURNEY
PREPARATION**

Surveying Your
Church's Landscape

Kay Kotan

the greatest
EXPEDITION

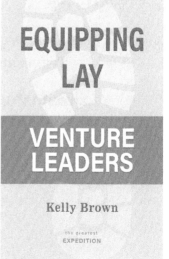

**EQUIPPING
LAY**

**VENTURE
LEADERS**

Kelly Brown

the greatest
EXPEDITION

MarketSquareBooks.com

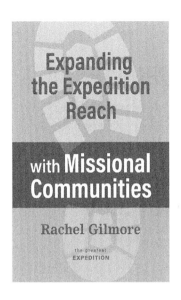

Expanding
the Expedition
Reach

with **Missional**
Communities

Rachel Gilmore

the greatest
EXPEDITION

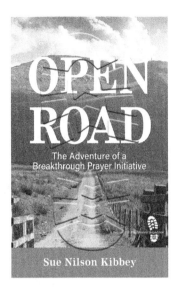

OPEN
ROAD

The Adventure of a
Breakthrough Prayer Initiative

Sue Nilson Kibbey

MULTI-SITE
MINISTRY

expanding the
Expedition Reach

KEN NASH
with Kristen Farrell

the greatest
EXPEDITION

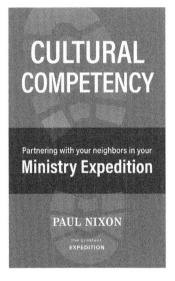

CULTURAL
COMPETENCY

Partnering with your neighbors in your
Ministry Expedition

PAUL NIXON

the greatest
EXPEDITION

MarketSquareBooks.com

EXPANDED THIRD EDITION!
New Resources, Activities, and Checklists

MISSION: POSSIBLE

A Simple Structure for Missional Effectiveness

Kay Kotan & Blake Bradford

MarketSquareBooks.com

IMPACT!

Reclaiming the Call of Lay Ministry

"What an 'IMPACT' for the Gospel of Jesus Christ could be made if every congregation studied this book and reclaimed the call of lay ministry!"
Mary Brooke Casad, Co-Author, *The Basics* series

Kay Kotan · Blake Bradford

MarketSquareBooks.com